Examination of the Revelation

By
Stephen Pope

About the Author

Stephen Pope began preaching at age 21 and has pastored the Calvary Baptist Church of Union Grove, North Carolina for more than 26 years. He studied at Hyles Anderson College and Andersonville Theological Seminary and graduated with a Bachelor of Science in Pastoral Theology. He has been married to his wife Tammy for 33 years and has been blessed with three wonderful children; Zach, Samuel and Hannah.

Pastor Pope is still very active in ministry and enjoys the challenge of pastoring, writing and being involved in public speaking.

All scripture quotations are taken from the King James Version Bible and are emboldened for personal emphasis.

Dedication

To a loving Savior, whose message I preach. Also, I would like to dedicate this book to a wonderful wife who constantly and lovingly encourages me to do more in the ministry of Christ. And I would be remiss if I did not mention the awesome people that I have had the privilege of pastoring at the Calvary Baptist Church for over twenty-six years.

Table of Contents

Introduction

Revelation. The mere mention of the word sparks immediate and imaginative thought. The hard truth is this, people are concerned and most curious about an *end of the world* scenario. Even those who claim to be non-believers can seem to discern that the thought of the world coming to an end is a very definite possibility, especially in these days of dictators and dangerous bombs.

The very word *Revelation* comes from the Greek word 'apokalypsis' or apocalypse, and it is defined as the expectation of an imminent cosmic cataclysm in which God destroys the ruling powers of evil and raises the righteous to life in a messianic kingdom. Could it really be true that man is headed for a real-life apocalypse? Dear Friend, it's not only true, but God is willing to reveal in great detail what will happen when this revelation comes to pass. Please understand that what we're about to study is not fairy tale or something derived from a Science Fiction book. The events we read about in the Book of Revelation are absolute reality. I agree that there are *some* symbols and types in this divinely inspired book, but just because an event is difficult for us to comprehend does not mean it should simply be tagged as a symbol. We're about to look into things that will be hard for the human mind to understand, but understandable or not, rest assured these things will come to pass. Revelation is one of those biblical books that spurs great curiosity, and if one is not careful, it can also bring great confusion. As we begin this journey, let me encourage every reader to breathe a prayer to the author of Revelation, the Holy Spirit, and ask Him to open your understanding. And now let me offer a slight disclaimer; this book is actually a rewriting of approximately two years' worth of Bible studies that I taught as a pastor a number of years ago. I make no claims to be a great Bible scholar, but I do believe that there will be some content within these pages that will be helpful to those interested in the end times. This book is completed in somewhat of an outline form. It is written in such a way as to make it easily understandable for the reader, while at the same time making it possible for the potential teacher or preacher to use it as a type of workbook in his communication with others. Please know that I am not expecting those who read this book to be blown away by these writings, but I do believe this book may supply you with some unique ideas that will assist you in general conversation and Bible communication.

In this first volume we will seek to discuss the opening of the Revelation, its introduction, and the events that surround the Rapture of the Church. May God bless you as we do an Examination of the Revelation.

Ready or Not, Here He Comes

As we begin this wonderful book of the Revelation of Jesus Christ we're reminded over and over again, that his coming appears close at hand. I believe the thing that makes this book so riveting for so many is that it describes in great detail the events that will happen when Christ does return; first for his church, then later as he comes to set up his kingdom on the earth. This is an appeal to all who will hopefully read further into these pages, that you will make sure of your own personal readiness for the return of our wonderful Lord. Many of the things you will read concerning the Rapture of the Church, the Tribulation Period, and the Second Coming of Christ will seem harsh, but keep in mind that these things unfold only after God has repeatedly extended mercy and grace to a world that seems bent on rejecting his pleas. I believe without a doubt that the coming of Christ is imminent. The stage seems to be setting before our very eyes, for all these things we will read about to come to pass. Let me begin by submitting some scripture references and a few simple reasons why I believe the Revelation is about to unfold.

1 The Revelation of Jesus Christ, which God gave unto him, to shew unto his servants things which must shortly come to pass; and he sent and signified it by his angel unto his servant John: (Revelation 1:1)

3 Blessed is he that readeth, and they that hear the words of this prophecy, and keep those things which are written therein: for the time is at hand. (Revelation 1:3)

11 Behold, I come quickly: hold that fast which thou hast, that no man take thy crown. (Revelation 3:11)

7 Behold, I come quickly: blessed is he that keepeth the sayings of the prophecy of this book. (Revelation 22:7)

12 And, behold, I come quickly; and my reward is with me, to give every man according as his work shall be. (Revelation 22:12)

20 He which testifieth these things saith, Surely I come quickly. Amen. Even so, come, Lord Jesus. (Revelation 22:20)

Some reasons I believe that the Revelation will unfold shortly: (What I believe is undeniable biblical proof)

1.) There will be an increase in knowledge and travel:

Da 12:4 But thou, O Daniel, shut up the words, and seal the book, even to the time of the end: many shall run to and fro, and knowledge shall be increased.

Notice what God told Daniel concerning the end of time - *Many shall run to and fro,* meaning an increase in travel. I recently read this statement – The earth is no longer a large place. In other words, it has become easier than ever to travel further and arrive there faster.

Knowledge shall be increased, which implies a boom of science and technology. It is amazing what has taken place in the area of technology even in the last 100 years. On March 10, 1876 – the first sentence was completed over a very primitive telephone, Alexander Graham Bell said these words, *"Watson, come here; I want you"*. Today you no longer need an actual phone line to make a call, one can stand practically anywhere in the world and dial a number, which will be connected by a system of satellites in a matter of seconds to connect your call. Cell phones seem to be in every hand. Years ago, it may have taken months for someone across the world to receive a letter in the mail, now it takes seconds through the means of *electronic mail.* In 1877 – the first phonograph was invented. In 1879 – the first lightbulb was invented. In 1913 – the first talking moving pictures were created. In the 1700's and 1800's people moved around by way of stagecoach and through improved roads traveled at a whopping 10 miles per hour. But in the last 100 years the automobile has been created and has transformed travel. We now have super airplanes that can potentially carry more than 853 passengers at one time. We have trains that travel 357 mph while people relax in comfortable seating or eat in a luxurious dining car. We have airplanes that zip through the air at Mach speed. In fact, America now has a plane that can travel at Mach 5 (3800 mph) and can potentially reach altitudes of 80,000 feet. In years gone by it took weeks and even months to cross the sea. For instance, the Pilgrims left Plymouth, England, on September 16 and arrived at Cape Cod on November 21 (36 days). Now we have the technology to board a supersonic jet and make a transatlantic flight from America to Europe in 3 hours. It is amazing what has happened in the last 100 years!

2.) There will be an intense move toward apostasy:

1 Now we beseech you, brethren, by the coming of our Lord Jesus Christ, and by our gathering together unto him, 2 That ye be not soon shaken in mind, or be troubled, neither by spirit, nor by word, nor by letter as from us, as that the day of Christ is at hand. 3 Let no man deceive you by any means: for that day shall not come, except there come a falling away (defection from the truth) **first, and that man of sin be revealed, the son of perdition; (2 Thessalonians 2:1-3)**

APOSTASY is the *formal disaffiliation from or abandonment or renunciation of a religion by a person, a moving away from the truth*. There is a steady move today away from the fundamental beliefs that once made America great. Things that used to be held and believed as right are being abandoned.

A} There is an abandonment of morals:

20 Woe unto them that call evil good, and good evil; that put darkness for light, and light for darkness; that put bitter for sweet, and sweet for bitter! (Isaiah 5:20)

We're living in a day when evil is made to look good and good is made to look evil. That which was clearly wrong just years ago is now tolerated and taught as normal and natural! We have new bills on Capitol hill promoting a transgender lifestyle. Immorality is now encouraged. Homosexuality is being promoted. Leaders are applauding the doing of wrong! According to one Christian publication, approximately 1 out of every 300 Americans over the age of 13 is infected with HIV, and by 1998, more than 375,000 Americans had died of AIDS, almost as many as the 400,000 Americans who died in World War II. In a recent internet article, it was even reported that a man married his dog. Pedophiles are seeking to gain the same rights as homosexuals. Abortion is being lobbied for and politicized. Drugs are being legalized!

B] There is an abandonment of the church:

Western cultures are facing a major problem, with 83.6 percent of America not attending a conventional church on a given weekend. In fact, some statistics tell us that in 1947 it was reported that 78 percent of Americans attended church, but in 1990 that number dropped to 20.4 percent. It has continued to drop and is now estimated that in the year 2050 only a little over 10 percent of the American population will attend any kind of church.

C} There is an abandonment of doctrine:

1 This know also, that in the last days perilous times shall come. 2 For men shall be lovers of their own selves, covetous, boasters, proud, blasphemers, disobedient to parents, unthankful, unholy, 3 Without natural affection, trucebreakers, false accusers, incontinent, fierce, despisers of those that are good, 4 Traitors, heady, highminded, lovers of

pleasures more than lovers of God; 5 Having a form of godliness, but denying the power thereof: from such turn away. (2 Timothy 3:1-5)

3.) Because of the future intentions of the Antichrist:

3 Let no man deceive you by any means: for that day shall not come, except there come a falling away first, and that man of sin be revealed, the son of perdition; 4 Who opposeth and exalteth himself above all that is called God, or that is worshipped; <u>so that he as God sitteth in the temple of God, shewing himself that he is God.</u> (2 Thessalonians 2:3-4)

Midway point into the Tribulation (3 1/2 years), the Antichrist will set himself up in the temple promoting himself as God, encouraging all to worship him. It will be at this point that many of the Jews seeing this action, will realize that this is not the true Messiah. But in order for this prophecy to happen, if the Antichrist will sit in the temple, a temple must be rebuilt in Jerusalem, due to the fact that the Romans totally destroyed the temple in 70 A.D. There is speculation and rumor circulating even now that plans are surfacing to rebuild the Temple in Jerusalem. This again is pointing toward the stage being set for the Tribulation to come.

The Background of Revelation

In gaining understanding of the Book of Revelation, it's important that we examine the background behind the book. Don't make the mistake of becoming impatient or getting in too much of a hurry in reading this wonderful book. If you miss the introduction that God gives us in the beginning of the book, you miss the importance of studying the book itself. So many are simply intrigued by the apocalyptic events, but they totally miss the reasoning of why God tells us about these events. If you miss the reason for the introduction simply because you want to read about the horrific events, then you might as well just watch a sci-fi movie or read an end of the world book! The beginning background lays a strong foundation for the rest of the entire book.

Some important things we notice concerning the background of Revelation:

1.) A Persecution:

I John, who also am your brother, and companion in tribulation, and in the kingdom and patience of Jesus Christ, was in the isle that is called Patmos, for the word of God, and for the testimony of Jesus Christ. (Revelation 1:9)

When John the Apostle pens this book, he is under the strong hand of persecution. The Emperor Domitian has banished John to the prison island of Patmos for his stand for Christ. Patmos was an island in the Aegean Sea, and it extends about 30 miles long. Patmos means *my killing*. Patmos was a very rocky island and known as sterile and infertile, nothing much was known to grow on this island; no type of crop that would necessarily sustain life. It would have been very hard to find food and possibly fresh water. The food that was available, would have been fought over by the other prisoners who were there. I'm just trying to emphasize this, because it's important for us to understand that John was not on vacation. The Apostle John was in one of the darkest times of his life. Basically, he was left there to die of starvation and exposure. Yet in the darkest of times, God chooses to give John one of the greatest books ever written.

Sometimes it is during the down times and the dark times that God chooses to do his greatest work. God is not giving *the Revelation* to a man who is living in the lap of luxury, but rather to a man who is suffering. When the going gets tough - don't quit! You don't know what God might be getting ready to do in your life. You have no idea how God may be getting ready to use you in a powerful way. I wonder how many people have quit, or backslid, or became bitter, right when God was preparing to do his greatest work in them?

9 And let us not be weary in well doing: for in due season we shall reap, if we faint not. (Galatians 6:9)

Therefore, my beloved brethren, be ye stedfast, unmoveable, always abounding in the work of the Lord, forasmuch as ye know that your labour is not in vain in the Lord. (1 Corinthians 15:58)

Thou therefore endure hardness, as a good soldier of Jesus Christ. (2 Timothy 2:3)

This new generation seems to know all too well about quitting. It seems many times when the first battle comes along they give up way too easily. Where are the *I-caners*? The *Survivors*? It has been rightly said - *I can is what makes a great man*! Someone used this little quip to describe the benefits of perseverance...

Two frogs fell into a deep cream bowl

one was an optimistic soul

but the other took the gloomy view

we shall drown, he cried, without more ado

so with a last despairing cry

he flung up his legs and he said – goodbye

quoth the other frog with a merry grin

I can't get out but I won't give in

I'll just swim round till my strength is spent

then I will die the more content

bravely he swam till it would seem

his struggles began to churn the cream

on the top of the butter at last he stopped

and out of the bowl he gaily hopped

What of the moral? tis easily found

if you can't hop out, keep swimming round

2.) A Presence:

I am Alpha and Omega, the beginning and the ending, saith the Lord, which is, and which was, and which is to come, the Almighty. (Revelation 1:8)

10 I was in the Spirit on the Lord's day, and heard behind me a great voice, as of a trumpet, 11 Saying, I am Alpha and Omega, the first and the last: and, What thou seest, write in a book, and send it unto the seven churches which are in Asia; unto Ephesus, and unto Smyrna, and unto Pergamos, and unto Thyatira, and unto Sardis, and unto Philadelphia, and unto Laodicea. 12 And I turned to see the voice that spake with me. And being turned, I saw seven golden candlesticks; 13 And in the midst of the seven candlesticks one like unto the Son of

man, clothed with a garment down to the foot, and girt about the paps with a golden girdle. 14-- His head and his hairs were white like wool, as white as snow; and his eyes were as a flame of fire; 15 And his feet like unto fine brass, as if they burned in a furnace; and his voice as the sound of many waters. 16 And he had in his right hand seven stars: and out of his mouth went a sharp twoedged sword: and his countenance was as the sun shineth in his strength. (Rev.1:10-16)

Notice what happens when John sees this presence...

17 And when I saw him, I fell at his feet as dead. And he laid his right hand upon me, saying unto me, Fear not; I am the first and the last:18-- I am he that liveth, and was dead; and, behold, I am alive for evermore, Amen; and have the keys of hell and of death. (Revelation 1:17)

These people amuse me who say they have had a *casual* encounter with Jesus Christ. They'll say something like, "Jesus came to see me the other day", or "I had a talk with the man upstairs", or "me and the man upstairs have an agreement". Listen, if you ever truly have an encounter with Christ, you'll know it, because your life will never be the same. We notice this encounter had an amazing effect on John the Apostle. Don't try to tell me you've had an encounter with Christ, and yet you're still living the same old way, with little to no change. If you ever have a close encounter with this presence I'm talking about, your life will never be the same. I'm reminded of John's writings in his first epistle when he spoke of personally coming into contact with Christ and how it is able to change a person.

1 That which was from the beginning, which we have heard, which we have seen with our eyes, which we have looked upon, and our hands have handled, of the Word of life; 2 (For the life was manifested, and we have seen it, and bear witness, and shew unto you that eternal life, which was with the Father, and was manifested unto us;) 3 That which we have seen and heard declare we unto you, that ye also may have fellowship with us: and truly our fellowship is with the Father, and with his Son Jesus Christ.

4 And these things write we unto you, that your joy may be full. (1 John 1:1-4)

2A} Notice the location of his presence?

12 And I turned to see the voice that spake with me. And being turned, I saw seven golden candlesticks; 13 <u>And in the midst of the seven candlesticks one like unto the Son of man</u>, clothed with a garment down to the foot, and girt about the paps with a golden girdle. <u>(Revelation 1:12-13)</u>

He is right in the midst or middle of the candlesticks. The implication here is clear, Jesus is in the center. In the same way, Jesus ought to be right in the center of everything we do in life; our preaching, our music, our ministry, our marriage, Christ should be the center of our life.

3.) A Purpose:

3 Blessed is he that readeth, and they that hear the words of this prophecy, and keep those things which are written therein: for the time is at hand. 4 John to the seven churches which are in Asia: Grace be unto you, and peace, from him which is, and which was, and which is to come;

and from the seven Spirits which are before his throne; 5 And from Jesus Christ, who is the faithful witness, and the first begotten of the dead, and the prince of the kings of the earth. Unto him that loved us, and washed us from our sins in his own blood, (Revelation 1:3-5)

Saying, I am Alpha and Omega, the first and the last: and, What thou seest, write in a book, and send it unto the seven churches which are in Asia; unto Ephesus, and unto Smyrna, and unto Pergamos, and unto Thyatira, and unto Sardis, and unto Philadelphia, and unto Laodicea. (Revelation 1:11)

God is speaking to the churches here. Because it is the churches that are to bear his message. It has now become the responsibility of the present-day local church to propagate this message of the kingdom of God. That message that says, Jesus is coming, and He will rule with a rod of iron. Life as we know it is coming to an end, so you had better trust Christ now, while saving grace is extended. Jesus is Prophet, Priest, and King. Christ is giving this revelation to the church, so the church can in turn carry this message to the world.

The Seven Churches

4 John to the seven churches which are in Asia: Grace be unto you, and peace, from him which is, and which was, and which is to come; and from the seven Spirits which are before his throne; (Revelation 1:4)

11 Saying, I am Alpha and Omega, the first and the last: and, What thou seest, write in a book, and send it unto the seven churches which are in Asia; unto Ephesus, and unto Smyrna, and unto Pergamos, and unto Thyatira, and unto Sardis, and unto Philadelphia, and unto Laodicea. (Revelation 1:11)

20 The mystery of the seven stars which thou sawest in my right hand, and the seven golden candlesticks. The seven stars are the angels of the seven churches: and the seven candlesticks which thou sawest are the seven churches. (Revelation 1:20)

Why would God take the time and space in a prophetic book, which reveals horrifying and apocalyptic events, to talk about Seven churches? After careful study and forethought, let me offer some ideas on these churches and why they are mentioned:

1.) We notice a Message:

These are more than likely actual churches existing in that day and this message was extended personally to each of them. The message of the Revelation has now been passed to the local churches in this present day. The church is to be the amplifier or the *Public Address system* for the message of the Gospel. It has become the commission of the church to carry this message of the Revelation. And notice the message that's emphasized in this book: Jesus is coming again, these things must shortly come to pass, the time is at hand, behold I come quickly, the Rapture is coming, tribulation is on the way.

2.) We notice a Model:

Some of these churches had to be reprimanded for what they had become, and I believe this is a relevant warning to all churches. Let's look at some examples:

A} Ephesus left its first love: (more than likely evangelism)

4 Nevertheless I have somewhat against thee, because thou hast left thy first love. (Revelation 2:4)

Notice the challenge from Christ to return to those first works.

5 Remember therefore from whence thou art fallen, and repent, and do the first works; or else I will come unto thee quickly, and will remove thy candlestick out of his place, except thou repent. (Revelation 2:5)

B} Pergamos allowed worldliness to creep in:

14 But I have a few things against thee, because thou hast there them that hold the doctrine of Balaam, who taught Balac to cast a stumblingblock before the children of Israel, to eat things sacrificed unto idols, and to commit fornication. (Revelation 2:14)

C} Thyatira became an ecumenical church: (embracing all religions)

20 Notwithstanding I have a few things against thee, because thou sufferest that woman Jezebel, which calleth herself a prophetess, to teach and to seduce my servants to commit fornication, and to eat things sacrificed unto idols. (Revelation 2:20)

I believe the Holy Spirit is challenging the church to look at this model and be careful not to fall into the same trap.

3.) We notice a Measurement: (a measurement of time)

What is the significance of these Seven churches? What was it that made these churches so special? Why would Christ choose these churches for a message and as a model? It's believed because each of these churches and the state they were in represents a different time in church history. Each church is like a measurement of time on the face of a clock, and they are in perfect order (just as the numbers on a clock) as to church history.

1- The Church of Ephesus: (this is believed to be the apostolic church and more than likely measured the period of time between AD 70 to AD 170)

2 I know thy works, and thy labour, and thy patience, and how thou canst not bear them which are evil: and thou hast tried them which say they are apostles, and are not, and hast found them liars: (Revelation 2:2)

John was thought to be the last surviving apostle. There were still some claiming to be apostles during this time, but in order to be an apostle it was necessary that you had personally saw the Lord.

1 Am I not an apostle? Am I not free? Have I not seen Jesus Christ our Lord? Are not ye my work in the Lord (1 Corinthians 9:1)

14 And he said, The God of our fathers hath chosen thee, that thou shouldest know his will, and see that Just One, and shouldest hear the voice of his mouth (Acts 22:14)

2- The Church of Smyrna: (this is believed to be the persecuted church and probably measured the period of time around A.D. 170 to A.D. 312)

8 And unto the angel of the church in Smyrna write; These things saith the first and the last, which was dead, and is alive; 9 I know thy works, and tribulation, and poverty, (but thou art rich) and I know the blasphemy of them which say they are Jews, and are not, but are the synagogue of Satan. 10 Fear none of those things which thou shalt suffer: behold, the devil shall cast some of you into prison, that ye may be tried; and ye shall have tribulation ten days: be thou faithful unto death, and I will give thee a crown of life. (Revelation 2:8-10)

Keep in mind that during this time Rome was a conquering force in the world and was staying very busy persecuting Christians. In fact, history tells us that in 40 B.C. there were 2000 crucified in one day simply for the entertainment of the Roman ruler. And that 40 years after the crucifixion of Christ Rome was said to have crucified 500 per day. It was suggested that the Emperor Nero would dip Christians in wax, impale their bodies on poles and set them on fire around his palace, and then cry "now you really are the light of the world".

3- The Church of Pergamos: (this is believed to be the state church and probably measured the period of time around A.D. 312 to A.D. 606)

14 But I have a few things against thee, because thou hast there them that hold the doctrine of Balaam, who taught Balac to cast a stumblingblock before the children of Israel, to eat things sacrificed unto idols, and to commit fornication. (Revelation 2:14)

This represents a time in history when the church became political (or in today's lingo *politically correct*). Things were changed in this church as a way to encourage worldly people to come in. A sensuous form of worship was adopted, the character of preaching was changed, clergy was exalted above the laity, and the priests were made to look like gods.

4- The Church of Thyatira: (is believed to be the Papal church and measured the time period of A.D. 606 to A.D. 1520 – or what we know as the *Reformation*)

18 And unto the angel of the church in Thyatira write; These things saith the Son of God, who hath his eyes like unto a flame of fire, and his feet are like fine brass; 19 I know thy works, and charity, and service, and faith, and thy patience, and thy works; and the last to be more than the first. 20 Notwithstanding I have a few things against thee, because thou sufferest that woman Jezebel, which calleth herself a prophetess, to teach and to seduce my servants to commit fornication, and to eat things sacrificed unto idols. (Revelation 2:18-20)

Jezebel (the wife of king Ahab) aided in bringing in Baal worship into Jerusalem. She killed every prophet of God possible and promoted the worshipping of images and bowing down to idols. The papal church began instituting the same type of worship (as they began introducing images and pictures for people to bow down to). But we know according to scripture that God is very displeased with such an act.

4 Thou shalt not make unto thee any graven image, or any likeness of any thing that is in heaven above, or that is in the earth beneath, or that is in the water under the earth:5 Thou shalt not bow down thyself to them, nor serve them: for I the Lord thy God am a jealous God, visiting the iniquity of the fathers upon the children unto the third and fourth generation of them that hate me (Exodus 20:4-5)

5- The Church of Sardis: (this is believed to be the dead church or formalistic church and it measured the time period of A.D. 1520 to A.D. 1750)

1 And unto the angel of the church in Sardis write; These things saith he that hath the seven Spirits of God, and the seven stars; I know thy works, that thou hast a name that thou livest, and art dead. 2 Be watchful, and strengthen the things which remain, that are ready to die: for I have not found thy works perfect before God. 3

Remember therefore how thou hast received and heard, and hold fast, and repent. If therefore thou shalt not watch, I will come on thee as a thief, and thou shalt not know what hour I will come upon thee. 4 Thou hast a few names even in Sardis which have not defiled their garments; and they shall walk with me in white: for they are worthy. (Revelation 3:1-4)

It was out of this church period that the Reformation took place. Bible believers (who were in this church) began to protest against the heretical teachings of the false church. False teachings like:

A} only the clergy could understand the scriptures:

This is exactly why the Sardis church period fought the translating of an English Bible. Many Bible believing men lost their life trying to translate the Bible into English. William Tyndale was known to have said, "I defy the Pope, and all his laws; and if God spare my life, ere many years, I will cause a boy that driveth the plough to know more of the scriptures than you do".

B} the selling of Indulgences:

An Indulgence was a document that stated your sins were forgiven. The more money you could invest secured you a larger indulgence.

6- The Church of Philadelphia: (this is believed to be the missionary church, or the true church, it measured the time around AD 1750 to AD 1900)

7 And to the angel of the church in Philadelphia write; These things saith he that is holy, he that is true, he that hath the key of David, he that openeth, and no man shutteth; and shutteth, and no man openeth; 8 I know thy works: behold, I have set before thee an open door, and no man can shut it: for thou hast a little strength, and hast kept my word, and hast not denied my name. 9 Behold, I will make them of the synagogue of Satan, which say they are Jews, and are not, but do lie; behold, I will make them to come and worship before thy feet, and to know that I have loved thee. 10 Because thou hast kept the word of my patience, I also will keep thee from the hour of temptation, which shall come upon all the world, to try

them that dwell upon the earth. (Revelation 3:7-10)

This is the time after the Reformation, where it seemed as if God opened a door for the gospel to be preached freely and deliberately.

7- The Church of Laodicea: (this is believed to be the apostate church and is the last church mentioned in what is known as *the Church Age*, its time period represents the present day)

I. What things does this church have in common with the modern-day church?

1.) This church is lukewarm:

15 I know thy works, that thou art neither cold nor hot: I would thou wert cold or hot. 16 So then because thou art lukewarm, and neither cold nor hot, I will spue thee out of my mouth. (Revelation 3:15-16)

Lukewarmness serves little purpose. No one likes to take a lukewarm shower or drink lukewarm coffee. No one desires a lukewarm heater on a cold day. Lukewarmness doesn't really heat you up if you're cold or cool you down if you're hot. This is exactly where most churches are today, they have just enough fire to keep people lukewarm. The preaching is lukewarm, the singing is lukewarm, the invitation is lukewarm, the youth group is lukewarm. Spiritually speaking they are just barely getting by.

2.) This church is loaded with complacency:

17 Because thou sayest, I am rich, and increased with goods, and have need of nothing; and knowest not that thou art wretched, and miserable, and poor, and blind, and naked: (Revelation 3:17)

The church today unfortunately seems unconcerned with growing, unconcerned with reaching more people, unconcerned about reaching out to other races or even someone that may be financially poor. There seems to be little concern about supporting missionaries and reaching the world with the gospel. It is a day when people are very unconcerned about attending services, and most church members are very satisfied with a mediocre spiritual journey. They seem unconcerned about responding to an invitation or contributing to an offering. What a sad state for the church to be in!

3.) This church has lost the presence of God:

20 Behold, I stand at the door, and knock: if any man hear my voice, and open the door, I will come in to him, and will sup with him, and he with me. (Revelation 3:20)

It's important for us to understand that this appeal was not made to the lost but rather to the church. In the Laodicean church, Jesus was standing on the outside wanting to come in. Sadly, many churches are there today.

The Rapture of the Church

20 Behold, I stand at the door, and knock: if any man hear my voice, and open the door, I will come in to him, and will sup with him, and he with me. (Revelation 3:20)

Notice, if you will, at the end of the church age - the location of Christ? Jesus is on the outside wanting to come in. Almost like a scorned lover unable to gain access to his house.

We use this as a verse for salvation but actually this is an appeal to the church.

A} Notice the appeal is to the Individual:

20 Behold, I stand at the door, and knock: <u>if any man hear my voice,</u> and open the door, I will come in to him, and will sup with him, and he with me. (Revelation 3:20)

The appeal here is to *any man.* Churches as a whole may not get serious about selling out to Christ and about inviting him in, but maybe there are some individuals who will.

As the present-day church turns toward apostasy and away from God, we now transition from a *message* to a *major event.* After Revelation chapter 3 - the church is not heard of again until all is fulfilled. This is because we believe the church is caught out immediately in chapter 4.

He that hath an ear, let him hear what the Spirit saith unto the churches. (Revelation 3:22)

4:1 After this I looked, and, behold, a door was opened in heaven: and the first voice which I heard was as it were of a trumpet talking with me; which said, Come up hither, and I will shew thee things which must be hereafter. 2 And immediately I was in the spirit: and, behold, a throne was set in heaven, and one sat on the throne. 3 And he that sat was to look upon like a jasper and a sardine stone: and there was a rainbow round about the throne, in sight like unto an emerald. 4 And round about the throne were four and twenty seats: and upon the seats I saw four and twenty elders sitting, clothed in white raiment; and they had on their heads crowns of gold. 5 And out of the throne proceeded lightnings and thunderings and voices: and there were seven lamps of fire burning before the throne, which are the seven Spirits of God. 6 And before the throne there was a sea of glass like unto crystal: and in the midst of the throne, and round about the throne, were four beasts full of eyes before and behind. 7 And the first beast was like a lion, and the second beast like a calf, and the third beast had a face as a man, and the fourth beast was like a flying eagle. 8 And the four beasts had

each of them six wings about him; and they were full of eyes within: and they rest not day and night, saying, Holy, holy, holy, Lord God Almighty, which was, and is, and is to come. 9 And when those beasts give glory and honour and thanks to him that sat on the throne, who liveth for ever and ever, 10 The four and twenty elders fall down before him that sat on the throne, and worship him that liveth for ever and ever, and cast their crowns before the throne, saying, 11 Thou art worthy, O Lord, to receive glory and honour and power: for thou hast created all things, and for thy pleasure they are and were created. (Revelation 4:1-11)

There has been no event of this magnitude since the flood of Noah's day. In fact, Noah's day was a picture of this major event - the Rapture of the Church.

I. Lessons about this Major Event:

1.) The Rapture will be a door opening event:

1 After this I looked, and, behold, a door was opened in heaven: and the first voice which I

heard was as it were of a trumpet talking with me; which said, Come up hither, and I will shew thee things which must be hereafter. (Revelation 4:1)

Notice some things that will happen when this door opens?

a} A trumpet will sound:

1 After this I looked, and, behold, a door was opened in heaven: and the first voice which I heard was as it were of a trumpet talking with me; which said, Come up hither, and I will shew thee things which must be hereafter. (Revelation 4:1)

16 For the Lord himself shall descend from heaven with a shout, with the voice of the archangel, and with the trump of God: and the dead in Christ shall rise first: (1 Thessalonians 4:16)

51 Behold, I shew you a mystery; We shall not all sleep, but we shall all be changed, 52 In a moment, in the twinkling of an eye, at the last trump: for the trumpet shall sound, and the

dead shall be raised incorruptible, and we shall be changed. (1 Corinthians 15:51-52)

b} A shout will occur:

1 After this I looked, and, behold, a door was opened in heaven: and the first voice which I heard was as it were of a trumpet talking with me; which said, Come up hither, and I will shew thee things which must be hereafter. (Revelation 4:1)

16 For the Lord himself shall descend from heaven with a shout, with the voice of the archangel, and with the trump of God: and the dead in Christ shall rise first: (1 Thessalonians 4:16)

c} A lift off will commence:

16 For the Lord himself shall descend from heaven with a shout, with the voice of the archangel, and with the trump of God: and the dead in Christ shall rise first:17 Then we which are alive and remain shall be caught up together with them in the clouds, to meet the Lord in the air: and so shall we ever be with the Lord. (1 Thessalonians 4:16-17)

The words "caught up" simply mean *to carry off by force* or *to snatch out or away*.

2.) The Rapture will be a grave opening event:

15 For this we say unto you by the word of the Lord, that we which are alive and remain unto the coming of the Lord shall not prevent them which are asleep. (1 Thessalonians 4:15)

The word *asleep* means to decease. The Bible quite often uses the word sleep to describe those who have passed away.

16 For the Lord himself shall descend from heaven with a shout, with the voice of the archangel, and with the trump of God: and the dead in Christ shall rise first: (1 Thessalonians 4:16)

When these deceased saints are raptured out to meet the Lord, I believe their physical graves will literally be opened up. Remember when Jesus finished his work on Calvary, and according to scripture then made His way to Paradise (that portion of Hades where the righteous saints were held) to once and for all redeem them to himself? As Christ took their spirits out of Paradise, it appears that their physical bodies actually came out of their graves.

50-- Jesus, when he had cried again with a loud voice, yielded up the ghost. 51 And, behold, the veil of the temple was rent in twain from the top to the bottom; and the earth did quake, and the rocks rent; 52 And the graves were opened; and many bodies of the saints which slept arose, 53 And came out of the graves after his resurrection, and went into the holy city, and appeared unto many. 54 Now when the centurion, and they that were with him, watching Jesus, saw the earthquake, and those things that were done, they feared greatly, saying, Truly this was the Son of God. (Matthew 27:50-54)

Physical graves opening up and resurrected bodies emerging - can you imagine what something of this magnitude will do to people psychologically? I wonder how the government will try to explain this away?

3.) The Rapture will be an eye-opening event:

You talk about chaos? Can you imagine when millions go missing in a single second?

Consider the carnage that will take place that day as jets are left with no pilots. A 747 for instance, that carries 524 passengers or a Boeing 777 that carries almost 48,000 gallons of jet fuel, now flying with a locked cockpit empty of pilots. Think about the buses, subways and trains that will be loaded with people on that fateful day, left with no driver. Tractor trailers loaded with 80,000 pounds of freight now barreling down the highway but left with no truck driver. Massive ships will be left without Captain or crew. Surgeries that will be in progress will instantaneously be left without surgeons. Law enforcement will be cut to skeleton crews, leaving anarchy to prevail. The Health profession will suffer great loses, needed doctors and nurses will vanish leaving hospitals grossly understaffed. And think about this, I believe that babies who have never reached the age of accountability will also be caught away during the Rapture. This means hospital nurseries all over the world will be left without babies. Can you imagine as unsaved parents that have just recently given birth, make a trip to the nursery to look at their new little bundle of joy, only to look through the glass at empty baby beds? It is without a doubt that this major event called the Rapture will alter this world in a moment of time.

Details about the Rapture

Although the term *Rapture* is not in your Bible, the teaching that supports this doctrine is. *Rapture* is defined as the carrying of a person to another place or sphere of existence. In this chapter I would like to discuss some things that will happen before, during and after the Rapture of the Church.

1.) Before the Rapture - there is no Warning:

When the Rapture of the Church finally does occur, it will come without any type of warning. In many communities out west, they have installed tornado sirens for the purpose of sounding an alarm (a warning if you will) in the event of an actual tornado. Most cell phones are now uploaded with a new emergency broadcasting system, which sounds an alarm if dangerous weather is approaching. But there will be no warning like this for the Rapture of the church.

In the Old Testament, Enoch's catching away was a type of the Rapture of the Church. And we notice that Enoch evidently had no formal warning that he was about to be caught away by the Lord.

18 And Jared lived an hundred sixty and two years, and he begat Enoch:19 And Jared lived after he begat Enoch eight hundred years, and begat sons and daughters:20 And all the days of Jared were nine hundred sixty and two years: and he died. 21 And Enoch lived sixty and five years, and begat Methuselah:22 And Enoch

walked with God after he begat Methuselah three hundred years, and begat sons and daughters:23 And all the days of Enoch were three hundred sixty and five years:24 And Enoch walked with God: and he was not; for God took him (Genesis 5:18-24)

Likewise, Elijah's catching away by a whirlwind into heaven was a type of the Rapture of the Church. Elijah knew something was going to happen, but he had no warning concerning the exact timing of his being caught away.

11 And it came to pass, as they still went on, and talked, that, behold, there appeared a chariot of fire, and horses of fire, and parted them both asunder; and Elijah went up by a whirlwind into heaven. 12 And Elisha saw it, and he cried, My father, my father, the chariot of Israel, and the horsemen thereof. And he saw him no more: and he took hold of his own clothes, and rent them in two pieces. 13 He took up also the mantle of Elijah that fell from him, and went back, and stood by the bank of Jordan; (2 Kings 2:11-13)

Finally, let us consider the ascension of Christ in the New Testament. When Jesus made His ascension back into heaven, the disciples that were present with Him seemed to have no idea that Jesus was about to be caught away.

8 But ye shall receive power, after that the Holy Ghost is come upon you: and ye shall be witnesses unto me both in Jerusalem, and in all Judaea, and in Samaria, and unto the uttermost part of the earth. 9 And when he had spoken these things, while they beheld, he was taken up; and a cloud received him out of their sight. 10 And while they looked stedfastly toward heaven as he went up, behold, two men stood by them in white apparel; 11 Which also said, Ye men of Galilee, why stand ye gazing up into heaven? this same Jesus, which is taken up from you into heaven, shall so come in like manner as ye have seen him go into heaven. (Acts 1:8-11)

2.) During the Rapture - there is no Waiting:

1 After this I looked, and, behold, a door was opened in heaven: and the first voice which I heard was as it were of a trumpet talking with

me; which said, Come up hither, and I will shew thee things which must be hereafter. 2 And immediately I was in the spirit: and, behold, a throne was set in heaven, and one sat on the throne. (Revelation 4:1-2)

51 Behold, I shew you a mystery; We shall not all sleep, but we shall all be changed, 52 In a moment, in the twinkling of an eye, at the last trump: for the trumpet shall sound, and the dead shall be raised incorruptible, and we shall be changed. 53 For this corruptible must put on incorruption, and this mortal must put on immortality. (1 Corinthians 15:51-53)

The word *moment* (in 1Cor.15) is defined as an atom of time or indivisible. I submit that the Rapture of the Church will take place so quickly that there will be no time to make a decision for Christ. There will be no time to call the pastor for spiritual counseling. There will be no time to hasten to the local church to make things right with God. The Rapture will occur and be over before people will be able to comprehend what has taken place.

Some things we notice during this immediate Rapture:

A) A door: (an open door)

This is a special event because the heavens are not always referenced as open (only at certain times). When we (as Christians) are raptured out of this world, we will be raptured *to and through* an open door. I believe that we will see the open door, but this door will not be visible to everyone. Let me offer a few examples of what may support this thought: In Mark's Gospel Jesus saw the heavens opened, but those around him did not

10 And straightway coming up out of the water, he saw the heavens opened, and the Spirit like a dove descending upon him:11 And there came a voice from heaven, saying, Thou art my beloved Son, in whom I am well pleased. (Mark 1:10-11)

In the book of Acts, the Deacon Stephen saw the heavens opened, but those around him clearly did not. In fact, Stephen's oppressors became enraged hearing him talk about heaven.

54 When they heard these things, they were cut to the heart, and they gnashed on him with their teeth. 55 But he, being full of the Holy Ghost, looked up stedfastly into heaven, and saw the glory of God, and Jesus standing on the right hand of God, 56 And said, Behold, I see the heavens opened, and the Son of man standing on the right hand of God. 57 Then they cried out with a loud voice, and stopped their ears, and ran upon him with one accord, (Acts 7:54-57)

Once again in the book of Acts we find an example of the Apostle Paul seeing the heavens opened, but it is clear that those around him did not.

3 And as he journeyed, he came near Damascus: and suddenly there shined round about him a light from heaven:4 And he fell to the earth, and heard a voice saying unto him, Saul, Saul, why persecutest thou me? 5 And he said, Who art thou, Lord? And the Lord said, I am Jesus whom thou persecutest: it is hard for thee to kick against the pricks. 6 And he trembling and astonished said, Lord, what wilt thou have me to do? And the Lord said unto him, Arise, and go into the city, and it shall be told thee what

thou must do. 7 And the men which journeyed with him stood speechless, hearing a voice, but seeing no man. (Acts 9:3-7)

So again, we will not simply be caught up immediately, but we will be caught up immediately to an open door.

B) A trumpet:

1 After this I looked, and, behold, a door was opened in heaven: and the first voice which I heard was as it were of a trumpet talking with me; which said, Come up hither, and I will shew thee things which must be hereafter. (Rev.4:1)

16 For the Lord himself shall descend from heaven with a shout, with the voice of the archangel, and with the trump of God: and the dead in Christ shall rise first:17 Then we which are alive and remain shall be caught up together with them in the clouds, to meet the Lord in the air: and so shall we ever be with the Lord. (1 Thessalonians 4:16-17)

52 In a moment, in the twinkling of an eye, at the last trump: for the trumpet shall sound, and

the dead shall be raised incorruptible, and we shall be changed. (1 Corinthians 15:52)

Many millions of the redeemed will hear the sounding of this great trumpet. It will be a wonderful summons to make our journey to that glorious place called heaven. But I submit that many living in this world will be unable to hear this trumpet sound.

25 Verily, verily, I say unto you, The hour is coming, and now is, when the dead shall hear the voice of the Son of God: <u>and they that hear</u> shall live. (*Implies some will not hear*) **26 For as the Father hath life in himself; so hath he given to the Son to have life in himself; 27 And hath given him authority to execute judgment also, because he is the Son of man. 28 Marvel not at this: for the hour is coming, in the which all that are in the graves shall hear his voice, (John 5:25-28)**

Radio and television signals fill (at any given time) almost every place you may be, but in order to hear (or receive) those signals you must have a proper receiver. On the day of the Rapture of the Church, those who have been

53

born again will possess the proper receiver to hear this great trumpet blow.

C) A voice:

1 After this I looked, and, behold, a door was opened in heaven: and the first voice which I heard was as it were of a trumpet talking with me; which said, Come up hither, and I will shew thee things which must be hereafter. (Rev.4:1)

16 For the Lord himself shall descend from heaven with a shout, with the voice of the archangel, and with the trump of God: and the dead in Christ shall rise first:17 Then we which are alive and remain shall be caught up together with them in the clouds, to meet the Lord in the air: and so shall we ever be with the Lord. (1 Thessalonians 4:16-17)

10 I was in the Spirit on the Lord's day, and heard behind me a great voice, as of a trumpet, (Revelation 1:10)

15 And his feet like unto fine brass, as if they burned in a furnace; and his voice as the sound of many waters. (Revelation 1:15)

What a voice God has! Christians won't have any problem hearing his voice on that day. But it stands to reason, with a voice as powerful as this, how do Christians miss hearing his voice today? The answer to this questions seems simple, they don't hear him because they don't want to hear him.

3.) After the Rapture - there is no Wishing:

2 And immediately I was in the spirit: and, behold, a throne was set in heaven, and one sat on the throne. (Revelation 4:2)

Immediately - John was caught up to a throne. It appears at least, that we will go straight from Rapture into the Judgment Seat of Christ. There will be no turning back, no restarts, no retakes, and no wishing I would have done differently. In the movie *It's a wonderful life,* George Bailey decides to commit suicide, but with the help of his guardian angel he is given a second chance at life. This is a delightful film and has a very happy ending, but rest assured, that this scenario will not happen after the Rapture. What we are going to do for the cause of Jesus Christ, we had better do now while we have time.

Parallels between the Rapture of Elijah and the Rapture of the Church

In 2Kgs.2:8-14 we find an Old Testament illustration of New Testament truth. This is the spectacular story of the prophet Elijah being caught away into heaven, without ever having to experience death. This amazing story, I believe is a picture of God's original plan before mankind fell into sin. Originally, man would have been able to fellowship with God without having to necessarily see death. But when man sinned, the penalty of death was imposed upon all men, requiring that they receive salvation and Christ' pardon of sin, before rapture into heaven and future fellowship with God can take place.

For the wages of sin is death; but the gift of God is eternal life through Jesus Christ our Lord. (Ro 6:23)

Wherefore, as by one man sin entered into the world, and death by sin; and so death passed upon all men, for that all have sinned: (Ro 5:12)

As we look into the story of Elijah being caught away into heaven – there are some wonderful parallels between the Rapture of Elijah and the Rapture of the Church:

1.) We notice an Angelic Ascension:

And it came to pass, as they still went on, and talked, that, behold, there appeared a chariot of fire, and horses of fire, and parted them both asunder; and Elijah went up by a whirlwind into heaven. (2Ki 2:11)

Someone may ask – What was this chariot of fire and horses of fire? No doubt, this was an angelic entourage coming to escort Elijah into heaven. Not necessarily an actual chariot, although it may have resembled a fiery chariot, but more than likely this was angels. Notice the next few verses that have remarkable similarities to what is described in Elijah's story.

Who maketh his angels spirits; his ministers a flaming fire: (Ps 104:4)

The chariots of God are twenty thousand, even thousands of angels: the Lord is among them, as in Sinai, in the holy place. (Ps 68:17)

And he rode upon a cherub, and did fly: yea, he did fly upon the wings of the wind. (Ps 18:10)

Someone has suggested that *chariot* is mentioned because Elijah went to heaven riding first class. Most of the common people in Elijah's day could not afford a horse, and most definitely not a chariot. Princes and kings, and those considered royalty, usually rode in chariots, and that's exactly how the prophet was caught away. Personally, I believe when Christians leave this world, they too will make that heavenly transition in a first-class manner. It's also very possible that Christians will be escorted into heaven by angels.

And it came to pass, that the beggar died, and was carried by the angels into Abraham's bosom: the rich man also died, and was buried; (Lk.16:22)

Death and the Rapture will pose no fear for the child of God. As an illustration, I thought about our church hospitality team. One of the responsibilities of our Hospitality Team at Calvary is to meet and greet people before they officially get into the church, and to make them feel welcome; to educate them concerning the church property, or escort them to their individualized Sunday School classes. We do this in an attempt to make people feel at ease and amazingly welcome. I believe that's exactly what God will do for us when we leave this world. A heavenly hospitality team will meet us and escort us into eternity.

2.) We notice an Announced Ascension:

Elijah (it would seem) knew his rapture was coming. Evidently, it had been announced to the prophet by the Lord that his rapture was soon to be.

9 ¶ And it came to pass, when they were gone over, that Elijah said unto Elisha, Ask what I shall do for thee, before I be taken away from thee. And Elisha said, I pray thee, let a double portion of thy spirit be upon me. (2Kgs.2:9)

We find that Elijah was apparently announcing it to others. He had evidently, shared this announcement with the sons of the prophets at two different locations.

3 And the sons of the prophets that were at Bethel came forth to Elisha, and said unto him, Knowest thou that the LORD will take away thy master from thy head to day? And he said, Yea, I know it; hold ye your peace. (2 Kgs.2:3)

5 And the sons of the prophets that were at Jericho came to Elisha, and said unto him, Knowest thou that the LORD will take away thy master from thy head to day? And he answered, Yea, I know it; hold ye your peace. (2 Kgs.2:5)

Dear Christian, we too should be sharing the news of the Rapture of the Church. Our daily message should be that Christ is coming and it is vital that we're ready to meet Him. In fact, it would appear that as a result of this message being propagated, the sons of the prophets were waiting to see this rapture of the prophet.

6 And Elijah said unto him, Tarry, I pray thee, here; for the LORD hath sent me to Jordan. And he said, As the LORD liveth, and as thy soul liveth, I will not leave thee. And they two went on. 7 And fifty men of the sons of the prophets went, and stood to view afar off: and they two stood by Jordan. (2 Kgs. 2:6-7)

We too should be waiting and looking for the Rapture to happen any time. Scripture challenges the child of God to be expectantly anticipating this special event.

Henceforth there is laid up for me a crown of righteousness, which the Lord, the righteous judge, shall give me at that day: and not to me only, but unto all them also that love his appearing. (2Ti 4:8)

Looking for that blessed hope, and the glorious appearing of the great God and our Saviour Jesus Christ; (Tit 2:13)

3.) We notice an Acknowledged Ascension:

As far as I can tell, Elisha was the only one allowed to see Elijah's ascension. In fact, it appears that Elijah may have taken himself and Elisha across the River Jordan, in order to get them out of sight of others.

11 And it came to pass, as they still went on, and talked, that, behold, there appeared a chariot of fire, and horses of fire, and parted them both asunder; and Elijah went up by a whirlwind into heaven.12 And Elisha saw it, and he cried, My father, my father, the chariot of Israel, and the horsemen thereof. And he saw him no more: and he took hold of his own clothes, and rent them in two pieces. (2 Kgs.2:11-12)

The sons of the prophets evidently did not see firsthand the ascension of Elijah, because they desired to form a search party of sorts, in an effort to locate the prophet, a project that Elisha knew was fruitless.

16 And they said unto him, Behold now, there be with thy servants fifty strong men; let them go, we pray thee, and seek thy master: lest peradventure the Spirit of the LORD hath taken him up, and cast him upon some mountain, or into some valley. And he said, Ye shall not send. (2 Kgs.2:16)

Elijah's rapture had taken place, but the sons of the prophets were unaware of his ascension. In the very same way, there is a good likelihood that the Rapture will take place, and most on earth will not comprehend that it has even happened.

Behold, I shew you a mystery; We shall not all sleep, but we shall all be changed, In a moment, in the twinkling of an eye, at the last trump: for the trumpet shall sound, and the dead shall be raised incorruptible, and we shall be changed. (1 Corinthians 15:51-52)

The word twinkling in verse 52 literally means *a stroke, or a beat.* The Rapture will begin and end as quickly as a physical heartbeat. There will be no time for an individual to respond. By the time one would think of a response, the event will be ended.

4.) We notice an Awkward Ascension:

When Elijah was raptured into heaven it caused a certain awkwardness to arise between he and Elisha.

a} it was awkward in Parting:

11 And it came to pass, as they still went on, and talked, that, behold, there appeared a chariot of fire, and horses of fire, and parted them both asunder; and Elijah went up by a whirlwind into heaven. (2Kgs.2:11)

Notice it suddenly parted Elijah and Elisha. Two people that loved and respected one another, were instantly separated. We find no place where they were able to say their goodbyes, or shake hands, or even embrace one last time. It was sudden, and we notice an element of sadness. In fact, the Bible records that Elisha rent his garment, which was at that time a symbol of sadness.

12 And Elisha saw it, and he cried, My father, my father, the chariot of Israel, and the horsemen thereof. And he saw him no more: and he took hold of his own clothes, and rent them in two pieces. (2 Kgs.2:12)

My dear friend, when the Rapture of the Church takes place, please understand, there will be no time to mend fences with others. There will be no time to make up or get right with God, and there will be no time to say your last good byes, or to even utter a quick prayer of repentance. What you and I are going to do with God, we had better decide to do now. No wonder the Bible proclaims in 2 Cor.6:2 "behold, now is the day of salvation."

b} it was awkward in Presence:

14 And he took the mantle of Elijah that fell from him, and smote the waters, and said, Where is the LORD God of Elijah? and when he also had smitten the waters, they parted hither and thither: and Elisha went over. (2Kgs.2:14)

When Elijah was caught away, it at least felt as if the presence of God had left. Much in the same way, when the Rapture of the Church takes place and the church is caught away, the presence of God (in the person of the Holy Spirit) will also be caught away. So practically speaking, one could correctly say, the presence of God will leave this world (at least as we know it now). Biblically speaking, it is God's Holy Spirit that is presently holding back the spirit of Antichrist from literally taking control in this world. But there will come a time (according to Scripture) when God's hindering Spirit will be taken out of the way, giving evil free reign on this earth.

For the mystery of iniquity doth already work: only he who now letteth will let, until he be taken out of the way. (2Th 2:7)

Can you imagine a world that feels totally void of the presence of God?

The Rapture and the Second Coming, what's the difference?

There are a number of future events still listed on God's prophetical calendar that should be of great interest to the Christian. Two such notable events are the Rapture of the Church and the Second Coming of Christ. If you are reading this book, you most certainly want to make sure that you are prepared and ready for the first of these crucial events, primarily the Rapture of the Church. Someone may ask, "How can I make sure that I am a part of this church that is raptured out? I believe without any doubt that the answer is found in the following scripture as Paul addressed the church of Thessalonica.

13 But I would not have you to be ignorant, brethren, concerning them which are asleep, that ye sorrow not, even as others which have no hope. 14 For if we believe that Jesus died and rose again, even so them also which sleep in Jesus will God bring with him. (1 Thessalonians 4:13-14)

The Bible is very clear about this subject, that if you and I want to be a part of this church, we must be believers; trusting in the finished redemptive work of Christ on the cross.

Often times the unsaved (and even Christians) make the mistake of getting these two prophetical events mixed up. At times a casual reader of scripture may unknowingly make them out to be the same event. But actually, the Rapture of the church and the Second Coming of Christ are two very different happenings. Granted, there are some things that seem similar about the two, but they are not the same. I would like to provide a few of those differences in this chapter.

1.) There is a difference in Direction:

In the Rapture of the Church, Christians are caught *up* to be with the Lord (in the air). But in the Second Coming, the Lord comes *down* (to the earth). Notice the following scripture concerning the Rapture:

16 For the Lord himself shall descend from heaven with a shout, with the voice of the archangel, and with the trump of God: and the dead in Christ shall rise first: 17 Then we which are alive and remain shall be caught up together with them in the clouds, to meet the Lord in the

air: and so shall we ever be with the Lord. (1 Thessalonians 4:16-17)

Now if you would, notice how scripture describes the Second Coming of Christ:

1 Behold, the day of the Lord cometh, and thy spoil shall be divided in the midst of thee. 2 For I will gather all nations against Jerusalem to battle; and the city shall be taken, and the houses rifled, and the women ravished; and half of the city shall go forth into captivity, and the residue of the people shall not be cut off from the city. 3 Then shall the Lord go forth, and fight against those nations, as when he fought in the day of battle. 4 And his feet shall stand in that day upon the mount of Olives, which is before Jerusalem on the east, and the mount of Olives shall cleave in the midst thereof toward the east and toward the west, and there shall be a very great valley; and half of the mountain shall remove toward the north, and half of it toward the south. (Zechariah 14:1-4)

2.) There is a difference in Decision:

Those who are saved before the Rapture are those individuals who made a decision to BELIEVE (or to accept Christ as Lord and Savior). *Notice the words in verse 13 – For if we believe.*

13 But I would not have you to be ignorant, brethren, concerning them which are asleep, that ye sorrow not, even as others which have no hope. 14 For if we believe that Jesus died and rose again, even so them also which sleep in Jesus will God bring with him. (1Thes.4:13-14)

16 For God so loved the world, that he gave his only begotten Son, that whosoever believeth in him should not perish, but have everlasting life. (John 3:16)

46 I am come a light into the world, that whosoever believeth on me should not abide in darkness. (John 12:46)

Now here is where we notice a significant difference between the *Rapture* and the *Second Coming*. Don't forget, those saved prior to the Rapture are saved by believing in Christ. But those who are saved after the Rapture, are those who make a decision to *believe* and also *endure* until the end. Because they waited to become believers, having now entered the Tribulation Period, they will be forced to couple their belief with endurance.

12 And because iniquity shall abound, the love of many shall wax cold. 13 But he that shall endure unto the end, the same shall be saved. (Matthew 24:12-13)

13 And ye shall be hated of all men for my name's sake: but he that shall endure unto the end, the same shall be saved. (Mark 13:13)

3.) There is a difference in Directive:

Christians will play a totally different role in these two major events in Bible prophecy.

A} In the Rapture - Christ is coming *for* His saints:

2 In my Father's house are many mansions: if it were not so, I would have told you. I go to prepare a place for you. 3 And if I go and prepare a place for you, I will come again, and receive you unto myself; that where I am, there ye may be also. (John 14:2-3)

B} In the Second Coming - Christ is coming *with* His saints:

14 And Enoch also, the seventh from Adam, prophesied of these, saying, Behold, the Lord cometh with ten thousands of his saints, 15 To execute judgment upon all, and to convince all that are ungodly among them of all their ungodly deeds which they have ungodly committed, and of all their hard speeches which ungodly sinners have spoken against him. (Jude 1:14-15)

14 And the armies which were in heaven followed him upon white horses, clothed in fine linen, white and clean. (Revelation 19:14)

So, we conclude from this, that in the Rapture of the Church, Christ will come *for* the saved. And in the Second Coming, He will come *with* the saved (to rule and reign on this earth).

4.) There is a difference in Decree:

Did you know in order for the Rapture to take place, scripturally speaking not one thing has to be fulfilled. In other words, the Rapture of God's saints could take place at any given moment. But on the contrary, before the Second Coming of Christ can occur, there are some things that must first come to pass:

1- Many shall come in my name (Matt.24:5)

2- Wars and rumors of wars (Matt.24:6)

3- Famines (Matt.24:7)

4- Pestilence (Matt.24:7)

5- Earthquakes (Matt.24:7)

6- Persecution and Martyrdom (Matt.24:9)

7- Bitter betrayal of loved ones (Matt.24:10)

8- False prophets shall deceive many (Matt.24:11)

9- The Love of many shall wax cold (Matt.24:12)

10- The Gospel shall be preached in all the world (Matt.24:14)

11- The Abomination of Desolation (Matt.24:15)

12- Mass exodus from Jerusalem (Matt.24:16)

13- Great Tribulation (Matt.24:21)

14- Additional false Christ's will arise (Matt.24:23-24)

15- The Sun will be darkened, the Moon will refuse to shine, and stars will fall (Matt.24:29)

16- The population of earth will see the Son of Man coming (Matt.24:30)

5.) There is a difference in Declaration:

51 Behold, I shew you a mystery; We shall not all sleep, but we shall all be changed, 52 In a moment, in the twinkling of an eye, at the last trump: for the trumpet shall sound, and the dead shall be raised incorruptible, and we shall be changed. (1 Corinthians 15:51-52)

The Rapture of the Church will take place secretly and quite suddenly; it will be without warning of any kind. In fact, when Paul uses the word *twinkling* in the aforementioned verse, it carries the implication of a *jerk* or *beat*; it comes from a word that means *sudden motion*. We are assured that the Rapture will come suddenly because scripture is careful to tell us that our Lord's coming will be similar to His ascension to heaven days after his resurrection. When Christ, from the mount, made His return to heaven, it appeared to be very unexpected by His disciples. And so will it be when He comes to rapture His saints.

9 And when he had spoken these things, while they beheld, he was taken up; and a cloud received him out of their sight. 10 And while they looked stedfastly toward heaven as he went up, behold, two men stood by them in white apparel; 11 Which also said, Ye men of Galilee, why stand ye gazing up into heaven? this same Jesus, which is taken up from you into heaven, shall so come in like manner as ye have seen him go into heaven. (Acts 1:9-11)

We should make no mistake about it, when the Rapture of the Church unfolds, people will undoubtedly be left behind. There will be no time to repent or make things right with a holy God. This world will be in a state of shock and disbelief - left without explanation.

But in contrast, the Second Coming of Christ will take place with Full disclosure. It will be everything but a closed event. When the Son of God returns after the Tribulation, it will most certainly be a worldwide announcement, bold and in the face of mankind.

26 Wherefore if they shall say unto you, Behold, he is in the desert; go not forth: behold, he is in the secret chambers; believe it not. 27 For as the lightning cometh out of the east, and shineth even unto the west; so shall also the coming of the Son of man be. (Matthew 24:26-27)

30 And then shall appear the sign of the Son of man in heaven: and then shall all the tribes of the earth mourn, and they shall see the Son of man coming in the clouds of heaven with power and great glory. (Matthew 24:30)

At Calvary Baptist Church, we hold to what is known as the *Pre-Tribulation* view of the Rapture. In other words, we believe that the Rapture of the church will take place before the Tribulation Period begins and prior to the Second Coming of Christ. Specifically, it will happen before the Antichrist sets up his kingdom and ruthless dictatorship and before the terrible time of chaos and great tribulation is released on this earth.

Some believe that the church will go into the Tribulation Period and be raptured out *Mid-Tribulation.* Or in other words, they believe that the church will be under the rule of the Antichrist for at least a time, and that they will experience at least a part of the horrific tribulations poured out on the world.

Still others believe that the church will go into the Tribulation and be raptured out *Post-Tribulation,* believing they will go all the way through before deliverance comes.

Why do we believe that the Bible teaches that the Rapture will occur before the Tribulation begins and prior to the Second Coming of Christ?

1.) We see the encouragement of Scripture:

17 Then we which are alive and remain shall be caught up together with them in the clouds, to meet the Lord in the air: and so shall we ever be with the Lord. 18 Wherefore comfort one another with these words. (1 Thessalonians 4:17-18)

Paul is saying, the message that our Savior is coming to catch us away, ought to encourage us. Think about it like this, if scripture told us that Christians are going into the Tribulation, and looking to suffer at the hands of the Antichrist, and most certainly facing great tribulation; I don't know if that would be very encouraging? Let me see if I can provide an illustration of sorts. What if you and your family were in a horrible car crash and several of your loved ones were severely injured. You hurriedly call 911 and emergency personnel confidently assure you that they will be there soon to provide aid; that would be an encouragement. But on the other hand, what if after placing that same call, emergency personnel told you that they were responding, but unfortunately it would be a great while before they arrived, too late to provide help to your wounded; would that still be an encouragement? Let's proceed a little further trying to make this point. Let's suppose you had someone breaking into your house during the night, at which time you nervously call the police for help. The police department assures you that they are only seconds away; that would be an encouragement. But, what if you made that same call and the police told you that their arrival would not be before tomorrow; would that be an encouragement or a discouragement? The Rapture of the Church is an encouragement because we understand that Christ will provide deliverance for His saints from this terrible time of tribulation and anguish.

2.) We see the Deliverance of the Savior:

10 Because thou hast kept the word of my patience, I also will keep thee from the hour of temptation, which shall come upon all the world, to try them that dwell upon the earth. 11 Behold, I come quickly: hold that fast which thou hast, that no man take thy crown. (Revelation 3:10-11)

10 And to wait for his Son from heaven, whom he raised from the dead, even Jesus, which delivered us from the wrath to come. (1 Thessalonians 1:10)

4 But ye, brethren, are not in darkness, that that day should overtake you as a thief. 5 Ye are all the children of light, and the children of the

day: we are not of the night, nor of darkness. 6 Therefore let us not sleep, as do others; but let us watch and be sober. 7 For they that sleep sleep in the night; and they that be drunken are drunken in the night. 8 But let us, who are of the day, be sober, putting on the breastplate of faith and love; and for an helmet, the hope of salvation. 9 For God hath not appointed us to wrath, but to obtain salvation by our Lord Jesus Christ, 10 Who died for us, that, whether we wake or sleep, we should live together with him. (1 Thessalonians 5:4-10)

The Tribulation Period will be a time of terrible wrath, and most who refuse the mark of the beast will be martyred by the Antichrist. It is a documented scriptural fact that millions will die. The Tribulation will be a time of terrible famine, disease and war. Large sections of the world's population will die quickly and inhumanely. We will get into some of the actual numbers in Volume 2, but it is believed that at one point during the Tribulation, that 115,000,000 people will die every single month. How could our Savior promise to deliver us from that kind of wrath, if we're destined to go through it?

3.) We see the absence of the Saved:

1 After this I looked, and, behold, a door was opened in heaven: and the first voice which I heard was as it were of a trumpet talking with me; which said, Come up hither, and I will shew thee things which must be hereafter. 2 And immediately I was in the spirit: and, behold, a throne was set in heaven, and one sat on the throne. (Revelation 4:1-2)

Before the Tribulation begins the church is mentioned over and over again. But once John is caught away, in what is believed to be a picture of the Rapture (*in chapter 4*), the church is not mentioned again during the entire Tribulation Period. In fact, in order for the Antichrist to begin setting up his kingdom on this earth, the church needs to be removed.

1 Now we beseech you, brethren, by the coming of our Lord Jesus Christ, and by our gathering together unto him, 2 That ye be not soon shaken in mind, or be troubled, neither by spirit, nor by

word, nor by letter as from us, as that the day of Christ is at hand. 3 Let no man deceive you by any means: for that day shall not come, except there come a falling away first, and that man of sin be revealed, the son of perdition; 4 Who opposeth and exalteth himself above all that is called God, or that is worshipped; so that he as God sitteth in the temple of God, shewing himself that he is God. 5 Remember ye not, that, when I was yet with you, I told you these things? 6 And now ye know what withholdeth that he might be revealed in his time. 7 For the mystery of iniquity doth already work: only he who now letteth will let, until he be taken out of the way. 8 And then shall that Wicked be revealed, whom the Lord shall consume with the spirit of his mouth, and shall destroy with the brightness of his coming: 9 Even him, whose coming is after the working of Satan with all power and signs and lying wonders, (2 Thessalonians 2:1-9)

Once the Spirit filled church is finally removed from the earth, absolute lawlessness will be prevail. Here is the important thing to remember, regardless of what you believe about when Christ is coming - HE IS COMING and ARE YOU READY?

The Most Noticeable Thing in Heaven

What a place heaven *is* right now! Heaven *will be* a great place when we arrive there one day, but please understand that heaven is a wonderful place *now*. Jesus ascended to this place called heaven not many days after his resurrection and has been preparing that place for all these many years. If the world was created in six days, can you imagine what Christ has completed in thousands of years?

A} In heaven there are mansions.

2 In my Father's house are many mansions: if it were not so, I would have told you. I go to

prepare a place for you. 3 And if I go and prepare a place for you, I will come again, and receive you unto myself; that where I am, there ye may be also. (John 14:2-3)

B} In heaven there are gates of pearl.

21 And the twelve gates were twelve pearls; every several gate was of one pearl: and the street of the city was pure gold, as it were transparent glass. (Revelation 21:21)

C} In heaven there is a street of gold.

21 And the twelve gates were twelve pearls; every several gate was of one pearl: and the street of the city was pure gold, as it were transparent glass. (Revelation 21:21)

D} In heaven there is a crystal river.

1 And he shewed me a pure river of water of life, clear as crystal, proceeding out of the throne of God and of the Lamb. (Revelation 22:1)

E} In heaven there is a tree of life.

2 In the midst of the street of it, and on either side of the river, was there the tree of life,

which bare twelve manner of fruits, and yielded her fruit every month: and the leaves of the tree were for the healing of the nations. (Revelation 22:2)

I believe the preceding verse implies that Heaven will be beautifully landscaped and arranged.

All these things will be so wonderful, but it is interesting that immediately following the Rapture, as John begins to give to us vivid details about heaven, he doesn't necessarily mention any of these magnificent things first. The thing immediately following the Rapture that *captures* John's attention is a throne. A throne is the very first thing John mentions seeing in heaven.

1 After this I looked, and, behold, a door was opened in heaven: and the first voice which I heard was as it were of a trumpet talking with me; which said, Come up hither, and I will shew thee things which must be hereafter. 2 And immediately I was in the spirit: and, behold, a throne was set in heaven, and one sat on the throne. (Revelation 4:1-2)

God is trying to send us a very important message here. In fact, it is mentioned 17 times in the next few verses. The very idea of a throne represents authority and brings to mind accountability. One can't help but walk into a court room without seeing the Judges Bench, that place that represents ultimate authority. Even to the extent that when the judge walks into the courtroom and is seated behind the bench, all present stand out of respect for that position of authority.

People think they can live half in and half out, just sort of playing church. They hardly give God a passing thought, they offer little dedication to the house of God, and then somehow, they believe they can die and enjoy all that heaven has to offer. I think it's important for us to understand that long before you and I see the street of gold, or the gates of pearl, or the heavenly mansions, or long before we're given a crown, we must come by a throne. Heavens throne is the first stopping point. There is no advancement until one sees the throne. There is no going to second base until you've come by first, and God's throne will be first.

I. Several things we notice about the Throne of heaven:

1.) The Occupation of the Throne:

Who is on this throne in heaven? The undeniable answer is most certainly this, God is on the throne as the triune God. (God the Father, Christ the Son, and the Holy Spirit)

A} God:

2 And immediately I was in the spirit: and, behold, a throne was set in heaven, and one sat on the throne. 3 And he that sat was to look upon like a jasper and a sardine stone: and there was a rainbow round about the throne, in sight like unto an emerald. (Revelation 4:2-3)

B} Spirit of God:

5 And out of the throne proceeded lightnings and thunderings and voices: and there were seven lamps of fire burning before the throne, which are the seven Spirits of God. (Revelation 4:5)

This is more than likely speaking of the 7 characteristics of the Holy Spirit. We find these mentioned in the prophecy of Isaiah.

2 And the spirit of the Lord shall rest upon him, the spirit of wisdom and understanding, the spirit of counsel and might, the spirit of knowledge and of the fear of the Lord; (Isaiah 11:2)

C} Christ: (the slain Lamb)

1 And I saw in the right hand of him that sat on the throne a book written within and on the backside, sealed with seven seals. 2 And I saw a strong angel proclaiming with a loud voice, Who is worthy to open the book, and to loose the seals thereof? 3 And no man in heaven, nor in earth, neither under the earth, was able to open the book, neither to look thereon. 4 And I wept much, because no man was found worthy to open and to read the book, neither to look thereon. 5 And one of the elders saith unto me, Weep not: behold, the Lion of the tribe of Juda, the Root of David, hath prevailed to open the book, and to loose the seven seals thereof. 6 And I beheld, and, lo, in the midst of the throne

and of the four beasts, and in the midst of the elders, stood a Lamb as it had been slain, having seven horns and seven eyes, which are the seven Spirits of God sent forth into all the earth. 7 And he came and took the book out of the right hand of him that sat upon the throne. 8 And when he had taken the book, the four beasts and four and twenty elders fell down before the Lamb, having every one of them harps, and golden vials full of odours, which are the prayers of saints. (Revelation 5:1-8)

1A} It's also worth mentioning that the Deacon Stephen saw the triune God on this throne:

55 But he, being full of the Holy Ghost, looked up stedfastly into heaven, and saw the glory of God, and Jesus standing on the right hand of God, 56 And said, Behold, I see the heavens opened, and the Son of man standing on the right hand of God. (Acts 7:55-56)

1B} The Bible definitely makes mention that God is a triune God.

7 For there are three that bear record in heaven, the Father, the Word, and the Holy Ghost: and these three are one. (1 John 5:7)

2.) Location of the Throne:

3 And he that sat was to look upon like a jasper and a sardine stone: and there was a rainbow round about the throne, in sight like unto an emerald. 4 And round about the throne were four and twenty seats: and upon the seats I saw four and twenty elders sitting, clothed in white raiment; and they had on their heads crowns of gold. (Revelation 4:3-4)

6 And before the throne there was a sea of glass like unto crystal: and in the midst of the throne, and round about the throne, were four beasts full of eyes before and behind. (Revelation 4:6)

Where is this throne? This is key; the throne is the center piece of heaven, and I believe it will be the focus of our attention for all of eternity. Everything will revolve around the throne of almighty God. Think about it like this, in cities around America there are landmarks that identify with a specific city. For instance:

Washington D.C. is known for the White House, Chicago is known for the Sears Tower, Seattle is identified by the Space Needle, South Dakota is famous as being the home of Mt. Rushmore, while New York's iconic landmark still is the Empire State Building. But in Heaven, amidst all of the glory and splendor, the focal point will be God's throne. For all of eternity we will be reminded that God is why we are in heaven. It was He who we were supposed to be living for while on earth. It is He who deserves all praise and glory. He is the ultimate reason for heaven.

17 And he is before all things, and by him all things consist. 18 And he is the head of the body, the church: who is the beginning, the firstborn from the dead; that in all things he might have the preeminence. 19 For it pleased the Father that in him should all fulness dwell; 20 And, having made peace through the blood of his cross, by him to reconcile all things unto himself; by him, I say, whether they be things in earth, or things in heaven. (Colossians 1:17-20)

People had better start preparing for that center piece of heaven now.

1) By learning to bow and humble themselves:

And when those beasts give glory and honour and thanks to him that sat on the throne, who liveth for ever and ever, 10 The four and twenty elders fall down before him that sat on the throne, and worship him that liveth for ever and ever, and cast their crowns before the throne, saying, 11 Thou art worthy, O Lord, to receive glory and honour and power: for thou hast created all things, and for thy pleasure they are and were created. (Revelation 4:9-11)

2) By learning to praise:

Dear Reader, when is the last time you got on your knees before God? When is the last time you raised your hands in praise and worship to the Lord of heaven? Notice Paul's challenge to Timothy in the proceeding verse.

8 I will therefore that men pray every where, lifting up holy hands, without wrath and doubting. (1 Timothy 2:8)

You may want to get in practice now for what's coming later.

3.) Explanation of the Throne:

What will take place at this heavenly throne? It is believed that judgment will take place here, but in two different forms or stages.

A} The Judgment Seat of Christ: (immediately following the Rapture)

1 After this I looked, and, behold, a door was opened in heaven: and the first voice which I heard was as it were of a trumpet talking with me; which said, Come up hither, and I will shew thee things which must be hereafter. 2 And immediately I was in the spirit: and, behold, a throne was set in heaven, and one sat on the throne. (Revelation 4:1-2)

4 And round about the throne were four and twenty seats: and upon the seats I saw four and twenty elders sitting, clothed in white raiment; and they had on their heads crowns of gold. (Revelation 4:4)

This will not be a judgment of sin, but a judgment of works. This is because as believers our sins were judged in Christ by His sacrificial death on the cross.

24 Who his own self bare our sins in his own body on the tree, that we, being dead to sins, should live unto righteousness: by whose stripes ye were healed. (1 Peter 2:24)

1 There is therefore now no condemnation to them which are in Christ Jesus, who walk not after the flesh, but after the Spirit. 2 For the law of the Spirit of life in Christ Jesus hath made me free from the law of sin and death. 3 For what the law could not do, in that it was weak through the flesh, God sending his own Son in the likeness of sinful flesh, and for sin, condemned sin in the flesh: (Romans 8:1-3)

But although we will not be judged for our sins, we (as Christians) will be judged according to our works and more specifically why we worked. (What did you do for Christ and why did you do it?)

10 But why dost thou judge thy brother? or why dost thou set at nought thy brother? for we shall all stand before the judgment seat of Christ. 11 For it is written, As I live, saith the Lord, every knee shall bow to me, and every tongue shall confess to God. 12 So then every one of us shall

give account (reasoning / motive) **of himself to God. (Romans 14:10-12)**

8 We are confident, I say, and willing rather to be absent from the body, and to be present with the Lord. 9 Wherefore we labour, that, whether present or absent, we may be accepted of him. 10 For we must all appear before the judgment seat of Christ; that every one may receive the things done in his body, according to that he hath done, whether it be good or bad. (2 Corinthians 5:8-10)

12 Now if any man build upon this foundation gold, silver, precious stones, wood, hay, stubble; 13 Every man's work shall be made manifest: for the day shall declare it, because it shall be revealed by fire; and the fire shall try every man's work of what sort it is. (My Paraphrase - WHAT SORT OF QUALITY) **(1Cor.3:12-13)**

It is the idea of Quality Control. Did you perform that Christian service because you loved me, or did you do it to be recognized and honored? Very simply stated, the Judgment Seat of Christ will be a *motive* judgment. What was the motive behind your Christian service?

14 If any man's work abide which he hath built thereupon, he shall receive a reward. 15 If any man's work shall be burned, he shall suffer loss: but he himself shall be saved; yet so as by fire. (1 Corinthians 3:12-15)

7 I have fought a good fight, I have finished my course, I have kept the faith:8 Henceforth there is laid up for me a crown of righteousness, which the Lord, the righteous judge, shall give me at that day: and not to me only, but unto all them also that love his appearing. (2 Timothy 4:7-8)

B} The Great White Throne Judgment: (at the end of the age)

This will most certainly be a judgment designed for those who have rejected Christ as Savior, as they will be judged one last and final time before being sentenced to the lake of fire.

11 And I saw a great white throne, and him that sat on it, from whose face the earth and the heaven fled away; and there was found no place

for them. 12 And I saw the dead, small and great, stand before God; and the books were opened: and another book was opened, which is the book of life: and the dead were judged out of those things which were written in the books, according to their works. 13 And the sea gave up the dead which were in it; and death and hell delivered up the dead which were in them: and they were judged every man according to their works. 14 And death and hell were cast into the lake of fire. This is the second death. 15 And whosoever was not found written in the book of life was cast into the lake of fire. (Revelation 20:11-15)

There is one final thing most certainly worth noticing about this throne in heaven; worship will be centered around the throne. It is apparent that at the close of the Judgment Seat of Christ, we will worship the Lord. And I believe that heaven will be permeated with a constant spirit of worship for our great and wonderful God.

9 And when those beasts give glory and honour and thanks to him that sat on the throne, who liveth for ever and ever, 10 The four and twenty

elders fall down before him that sat on the throne, and worship him that liveth for ever and ever, and cast their crowns before the throne, saying, 11 Thou art worthy, O Lord, to receive glory and honour and power: for thou hast created all things, and for thy pleasure they are and were created. (Revelation 4:9-11)

The Judgment Seat of Christ

It is believed that Chapter four of Revelation is a reference to the Rapture of the church. Then as we mentioned in the preceding chapter, John now caught away into heaven, immediately sees a throne.

2 And immediately I was in the spirit: and, behold, a throne was set in heaven, and one sat on the throne. (Revelation 4:2)

We believe it is at this point that the Judgment Seat of Christ takes place. We also notice around the throne are positioned twenty four other seats.

4 And round about the throne were four and twenty seats: and upon the seats I saw four and twenty elders sitting, clothed in white raiment; and they had on their heads crowns of gold. (Revelation 4:4)

These twenty-four seats are a picture of the Redeemed. By Redeemed I believe it speaks of the Twelve tribes of Israel (a picture of those believers that looked forward to the coming Messiah) and also the Twelve Apostles of Christ (a picture of those believers who reflected back on the Messiah's finished work on Calvary). And notice the Redeemed are clothed in white raiment and wearing crowns. This white raiment is a picture of righteousness issued by God himself.

And to her was granted that she should be arrayed in fine linen, clean and white: for the fine linen is the righteousness of saints. (Revelation 19:8)

And the armies which were in heaven followed him upon white horses, clothed in fine linen, white and clean. (Revelation 19:14)

If I could provide an illustration that may lend some clarity to this thought; when citizens volunteered for military service, they were issued a regulation uniform because of their willingness to sign up. Understandably, not just anyone gets to wear a distinguished U.S. military uniform. But only those who are willing to pay the sacrifice of defending their countries constitution. Much in the same way, not everyone will be allowed to wear this white raiment distributed in heaven. It will be reserved for those who made the choice to receive Christ as their personal Savior.

4 And round about the throne were four and twenty seats: and upon the seats I saw four and twenty elders sitting, clothed in white raiment;

and they had on their heads crowns of gold. (Revelation 4:4)

These crowns, white raiment and seats (or thrones) are a picture of rewards and authority that is awarded to those present at the Judgment Seat of Christ. It is not necessarily that we will wear crowns all of the time in heaven, but that we will at least have access to crowns. The Queen of England doesn't wear a crown all of the time, but she does have access to a crown because of her position and authority.

2 Do ye not know that the saints shall judge the world? and if the world shall be judged by you, are ye unworthy to judge the smallest matters? 3 Know ye not that we shall judge angels? how much more things that pertain to this life? (1 Corinthians 6:2-3)

Behold, a king shall reign in righteousness, and princes shall rule in judgment. (Isaiah 32:1)

And I saw thrones, and they sat upon them, and judgment was given unto them: and I saw the souls of them that were beheaded for the witness of Jesus, and for the word of God, and

which had not worshipped the beast, neither his image, neither had received his mark upon their foreheads, or in their hands; and they lived and reigned with Christ a thousand years. (Revelation 20:4)

I. Some lessons about the Judgment Seat of Christ:

11 For other foundation can no man lay than that is laid, which is Jesus Christ. 12 Now if any man build upon this foundation gold, silver, precious stones, wood, hay, stubble; 13 Every man's work shall be made manifest: for the day shall declare it, because it shall be revealed by fire; and the fire shall try every man's work of what sort it is. 14 If any man's work abide which he hath built thereupon, he shall receive a reward. 15 If any man's work shall be burned, he shall suffer loss: but he himself shall be saved; yet so as by fire. (1 Corinthians 3:11-15)

1.) The Judgment Seat of Christ - is not a sin judgment:

Our sins were judged in Christ on the cross.

24 Who his own self bare our sins in his own body on the tree, that we, being dead to sins, should live unto righteousness: by whose stripes ye were healed. (1 Peter 2:24)

21 For he hath made him to be sin for us, who knew no sin; that we might be made the righteousness of God in him. (2 Corinthians 5:21)

1 There is therefore now no condemnation to them which are in Christ Jesus, who walk not after the flesh, but after the Spirit. (Romans 8:1)

The debt was paid in full. Past, present and future. And for those reading this book, all of our sins were future when Christ died on the cross. Which means He paid for every sin ever committed.

11 But Christ being come an high priest of good things to come, by a greater and more perfect tabernacle, not made with hands, that is to say, not of this building; 12 Neither by the blood of goats and calves, but by his own blood he entered in once into the holy place, having

obtained eternal redemption for us (Hebrews 9:11-12)

24 For Christ is not entered into the holy places made with hands, which are the figures of the true; but into heaven itself, now to appear in the presence of God for us:25 Nor yet that he should offer himself often, as the high priest entereth into the holy place every year with blood of others; 26 For then must he often have suffered since the foundation of the world: but now once in the end of the world hath he appeared to put away sin by the sacrifice of himself. 27 And as it is appointed unto men once to die, but after this the judgment:28 So Christ was once offered to bear the sins of many; and unto them that look for him shall he appear the second time without sin unto salvation. (Hebrews 9:24-28)

Eternal punishment is not mentioned at this judgment, because this is saved people.

15 If any man's work shall be burned, he shall suffer loss: but he himself shall be saved; yet so as by fire. (1 Corinthians 3:15)

Note: Some will be saved *yet so as by fire.* Which means that there will be some people in heaven that barely make it in. They were saved by the grace of God, but will have no works of any kind to show for their love and dedication to Christ. Possibly, they were saved right at the point of death, and therefore missed the opportunity of living a victorious life for Christ and bringing glory to Him.

2.) The Judgment Seat of Christ is a saved judgment:

It is a judgment reserved only for Christians. Not every man will be at this judgment, because it seems to take place right after the Rapture of the church. This means that millions will still be on earth during this time. Immediately following the Rapture, we see the Redeemed given seats (or thrones) and arrayed in white (representing the righteous acts of the saints). Hence, the Judgment Seat of Christ must take place right after the Rapture of the church. So only saved people will be present.

10 But why dost thou judge thy brother? or why dost thou set at nought thy brother? for we shall

all stand before the judgment seat of Christ. 11 For it is written, As I live, saith the Lord, every knee shall bow to me, and every tongue shall confess to God. 12 So then every one of us shall give account of himself to God. (Romans 14:10-12)

Paul is speaking to Christians here. Notice what Paul spoke of when writing to the church of Corinth:

8 We are confident, I say, and willing rather to be absent from the body, and to be present with the Lord. 9 Wherefore we labour, that, whether present or absent, we may be accepted of him. 10 For we must all appear before the judgment seat of Christ; that every one may receive the things done in his body, according to that he hath done, whether it be good or bad. (2 Corinthians 5:8-10)

3.) The Judgment Seat of Christ is a sort judgment:

13 Every man's work shall be made manifest: for the day shall declare it, because it shall be revealed by fire; and the fire shall try every

man's work of what sort it is. (1 Corinthians 3:13)

It is a judgment of works and what sort or manner they are? This judgment will reveal whether our works are gold, silver, precious stones? Or wood, hay, stubble?

a} Jesus has laid the foundation:

11 For other foundation can no man lay than that is laid, which is Jesus Christ. (1 Corinthians 3:11)

b} We build upon that foundation:

12 Now if any man build upon this foundation gold, silver, precious stones, wood, hay, stubble; (1 Corinthians 3:12)

c} At the Judgment Seat - what we have built will be tried by fire:

If it withstands the fire, the Christian is rewarded. If it burns, the Christian loses his reward. If your works are represented as gold, silver, precious stones, the implication is that these are items that cannot be consumed by fire. So, someone may ask, what determines this?

(What determines if your works are considered to be gold, silver or precious stones?) And the answer is - What sort they are. What was the motive behind the works that you performed for Christ? Did you do it for Christ sake? Did you do what you did for his glory, for his pleasing? Or did you do it to be seen of men? This makes all the difference in eternity.

1 Take heed that ye do not your alms before men, to be seen of them: otherwise ye have no reward of your Father which is in heaven. 2 Therefore when thou doest thine alms, do not sound a trumpet before thee, as the hypocrites do in the synagogues and in the streets, that they may have glory of men. Verily I say unto you, They have their reward. 3 But when thou doest alms, let not thy left hand know what thy right hand doeth:4 That thine alms may be in secret: and thy Father which seeth in secret himself shall reward thee openly. (Matthew 6:1-4)

5 And when thou prayest, thou shalt not be as the hypocrites are: for they love to pray standing in the synagogues and in the corners of the streets, that they may be seen of men.

Verily I say unto you, They have their reward. 6 But thou, when thou prayest, enter into thy closet, and when thou hast shut thy door, pray to thy Father which is in secret; and thy Father which seeth in secret shall reward thee openly. (Matthew 6:5-6)

4.) The Judgment Seat of Christ will be a sad judgment:

You and I are going to want to receive rewards, so we will have something to worship Christ with when we finally stand in His presence in heaven. Notice what chapter four tells us will happen once we arrive to our heavenly home:

8 And the four beasts had each of them six wings about him; and they were full of eyes within: and they rest not day and night, saying, Holy, holy, holy, Lord God Almighty, which was, and is, and is to come. 9 And when those beasts give glory and honour and thanks to him that sat on the throne, who liveth for ever and ever, 10 The four and twenty elders fall down before him that sat on the throne, and worship him that liveth for ever and ever, and cast their

crowns before the throne, saying, 11 Thou art worthy, O Lord, to receive glory and honour and power: for thou hast created all things, and for thy pleasure they are and were created. (Revelation 4:8-11)

Can you imagine having nothing to give to the Lord while all of heaven is adoring him with gifts? After Christ gave us everything and we have nothing to give him in return. Think of the embarrassment and the shame. It would be like showing up to a birthday party, and every single person having a present for the honored person, *except you*. Maybe this is why John mentions facing the appearance of the Lord one day with confidence.

28 And now, little children, abide in him; that, when he shall appear, we may have confidence, and not be ashamed before him at his coming. (1 John 2:28)

I would like to thank you for reading this first installment of *An Examination of the Revelation.* In our next volume we will plan on discussing the Seven sealed book and all that will transpire during the actual days of the Tribulation Period; it's destined to be an inspiring study.

Made in the USA
San Bernardino, CA
16 October 2018